WILD AND WHALE

Written by Paul Shipton
Illustrated by Shahab Shamshirsaz

Wilbur Willis was a wildlife expert on telly.
He was looking for whales to film.

Cherie was the person who filmed him for his show.

"We are looking for a whale that few people have seen," said Wilbur. "It is a great white whale."

Suddenly a huge white tail came up out of the water.

"It's the great white whale!" whooped Wilbur. "Now is our chance!"

But the white tail whooshed back under the waves.

While Cherie was filming one way, the white whale whooshed out of the water behind them.

It whizzed through the air and sank down into the water.

"You missed it *again*!" Wilbur whined.

After that, the boat was still for a long while.

Cherie whirled around to film, but the whale sank under the water again.

"WHY?" Wilbur wailed.

"Why can't you film that whale?"

"Don't whinge," Cherie whispered. "The white whale is right behind you." Wilbur stood up slowly.

But the whale whacked its tail on the water. WHAM!
Water splashed onto the little boat.

Wilbur slipped and . . . he fell right in the water.

"I think I've got it!" whooped Cherie.

Wilbur *did* win a prize, but not for the best wildlife show on telly. It was for the best comedy!